Free To Be Me

Leadership Guide for Girls

IMAGINE

Journal

Free To Be Me

Leadership Guide for Girls

Journal

ISBN-13:978-1537389981

ISBN-10:153738998X

_"You are the one that possesses the keys to your being.
You carry the passport to your own happiness."_
Diane von Furstenberg

"When the whole world is silent, even one voice becomes powerful."
Malala Yousafzai

"*Make the most of yourself by fanning the tiny, inner sparks of possibility into flames of achievement.*"
Golda Meir

"Knowing what must be done does away with fear."
Rosa Parks

"*I didn't get there by wishing for it or hoping for it,
but by working for it.*"
Estée Lauder

"Power's not given to you. You have to take it."
Beyoncé Knowles Carter

_____

_____

_____

_____

_____

_____

_____

_____

_____

_____

_____

_____

_____

_____

_____

_____

*"The most difficult thing is the decision to act, the rest
is merely tenacity."*
Amelia Earhart

"*The difference between successful people and others is how long they spend time feeling sorry for themselves.*"
Barbara Corcoran

_____

_____

_____

_____

_____

_____

_____

_____

_____

_____

_____

_____

_____

_____

_____

_____

_____

_____

"You can waste your lives drawing lines. Or you can live your life crossing them."
Shonda Rhimes

"*I'd rather regret the things I've done than regret the things I haven't done.*"
Lucille Ball

"I hope the fathers and mothers of little girls will look
at them and say 'yes, women can.'"
Dilma Rousseff

*"If you don't like the road you're walking,
start paving another one."*
Dolly Parton

_____

_____

_____

_____

_____

_____

_____

_____

_____

_____

_____

_____

_____

_____

_____

_____

"You can't give up! If you give up, you're like everybody else."
Chris Evert

_____

_____

_____

_____

_____

_____

_____

_____

_____

_____

_____

_____

_____

_____

_____

_____

_____

_____

_____

_____

_____

_____

_____

_____

_____

_____

_____

_____

_____

_____

_____

_____

_____

_____

_____

_____

_____

_____

*"No matter how difficult and painful it may be,
nothing sounds as good to the soul as the truth."*
Martha Beck

"*Done is better than perfect.*"
Sheryl Sandberg

"One of the secrets to staying young is to always do things you don't know how to do, to keep learning."
Ruth Reichl

"*Step out of the history that is holding you back. Step into the new story you are willing to create.*"
Oprah Winfrey

"What you do makes a difference, and you have to decide what kind of difference you want to make."
Jane Goodall

"A good compromise is one where everybody
makes a contribution."
Angela Merkel

_____

_____

_____

_____

_____

_____

_____

_____

_____

_____

_____

_____

_____

_____

_____

_____

_____

"A strong woman is a woman determined to do something others are determined not be done."
Marge Piercy

"*I choose to make the rest of my life the best of my life.*"
Louise Hay

"In order to be irreplaceable one must always be different."
Coco Chanel

"The question isn't who is going to let me; it's who is going to stop me."
Ayn Rand

"*Spread love everywhere you go. Let no one ever come to you without leaving happier.*"
Mother Teresa

"Take criticism seriously, but not personally. If there is truth or merit in the criticism, try to learn from it. Otherwise, let it roll right off you."
Hillary Clinton

"When we speak we are afraid our words will not be heard or welcomed. But when we are silent, we are still afraid. So it is better to speak."
Audre Lorde

_____

_____

_____

_____

_____

_____

_____

_____

_____

_____

_____

_____

_____

_____

_____

_____

_____

_____

"Learn from the mistakes of others. You can't live long enough to make them all yourself."
Eleanor Roosevelt

"*Above all, be the heroine of your life, not the victim.*"
Nora Ephron

"It's one of the greatest gifts you can give yourself, to forgive. Forgive everybody."
Maya Angelou

"*Change your life today. Don't gamble on the future,
act now, without delay.*"
Simone de Beauvoir

"*Doubt is a killer. You just have to know who you are and what you stand for.*"
Jennifer Lopez

"You can be the lead in your own life."
Kerry Washington

_____

_____

_____

_____

_____

_____

_____

_____

_____

_____

_____

_____

_____

_____

_____

_____

_____

_____

"You can't please everyone, and you can't make everyone like you."
Katie Couric

"*Owning our story can be hard but not nearly as difficult as spending our lives running from it.*"
Brene Brown

_____

_____

_____

_____

_____

_____

_____

_____

_____

_____

_____

_____

_____

_____

_____

_____

_____

_____

"I do not try to dance better than anyone else. I only try to dance better than myself."
Arianna Huffington

_____

_____

_____

_____

_____

_____

_____

_____

_____

_____

_____

_____

_____

_____

_____

_____

_____

_____

"If you don't get out of the box you've been raised in,
you won't understand how much bigger the world is."
Angelina Jolie

"*Everyone shines, given the right lighting.*"
Susan Cain

"*You can't be that kid standing at the top of the waterslide, overthinking it. You have to go down the chute.*"
Tina Fey

"If you just set out to be liked, you would be prepared to compromise on anything at any time, and you would achieve nothing."
Margaret Thatcher

_____
_____
_____
_____
_____
_____
_____
_____
_____
_____
_____
_____
_____
_____
_____
_____
_____

"The challenge is not to be perfect...it's to be whole."
Jane Fonda

"*Don't look at your feet to see if you are doing it right. Just dance.*"
Anne Lamott

"There are two kinds of people, those who do the work and those who take the credit. Try to be in the first group; there is less competition there."
Indira Gandhi

"*You have trust in what you think. If you splinter
yourself and try to please everyone, you can't.*"
Annie Leibovitz

_____

_____

_____

_____

_____

_____

_____

_____

_____

_____

_____

_____

_____

_____

_____

_____

_____

"We do not need magic to change the world, we carry all the power we need inside ourselves already: we have the power to imagine better."

J.K. Rowling

"We need to start work with the idea that we're going to learn every day. I learn, even at my position, every single day."
Chanda Kochhar

"Style is a way to say who you are without having to speak."
Rachel Zoe

_____

_____

_____

_____

_____

_____

_____

_____

_____

_____

_____

_____

_____

_____

_____

_____

_____

_____

_____

"I learned compassion from being discriminated against. Everything bad that's ever happened to me has taught me compassion."
Ellen DeGeneres

"Don't live life in the past lane."
Samantha Ettus

"*Many receive advice, only the wise profit from it.*"
Harper Lee

_____
_____
_____
_____
_____
_____
_____
_____
_____
_____
_____
_____
_____
_____
_____
_____
_____
_____
_____

"Hold your head and your standards high even as people or circumstances try to pull you down."
Tory Johnson

Made in the USA
Columbia, SC
10 November 2018